Leadership Singularity

How Marketing Can Save The World

John Caswell

Jonathan Cook

Virginie Glaenzer

Patrick Novak

DEDICATION

This book is dedicated to the first responders, doctors, and business leaders who knew from the start, that the only way to save humanity was for all of us to do our part selflessly and collectively. As long as we are humans on earth, we'll always be "in this together". Hopefully, by the time you finish reading this, you'll be inspired to take responsibility at whatever corporate level you're in to meaningfully contribute to ethical leadership and marketing practices that promote the stability and wellbeing of your community, coworkers, employees and customers.

Contents

NORTHSTAR

Leadership Principles In A Pandemic

This book started as a blog, by author Virginie Glaenzer, that turned into a tweet, that got a comment, that brought together four strangers from entirely different backgrounds just weeks before the worldwide COVID-19 virus drastically changed how humanity conducted commerce, marketing, and corporate leadership.

The authors ***initially*** came together before the pandemic. They aimed to solve the critical question currently plaguing international economies and all human existence: *"How can a global coalition of business leaders build trust, inspire confidence, and expand ethics-infused commerce through innovative marketing strategies?"*

We were seeking to address this issue before the pandemic. When it struck, it only added to the fire within each of us. Interestingly it led to us re-validating our market research and initial hypothesis in ways that we couldn't have imagined.

In this book, we lay bare a few of the long-held "truths". We unpack some of the evolutionary psychology that led us to our current marketing and leadership practices. We deconstruct the restrictive "scaffolding" that maintains the obsolete system. A system that no longer promotes anything like the social fabric we need for the sustainability of our planet.

The current reality has us all in a frantic search for adaptable and scalable solutions. The authors put the context surrounding the pandemic under a microscope to engineer, improve, and launch a new framework built for the future.

It shouldn't have taken a damn virus to show us just how sick our corporate dysfunction was. Luckily, there's a community of cutting-edge leaders, marketers, and practitioners prepared to provide a cure.

As cultural norms change daily, no government or corporate entity will have all the answers. *Leadership Singularity* offers a new leadership framework and emerging principles through which we can build new corporate strategies that create better companies for humanity.

Our framework won't return business practices to a pre-pandemic state. Instead, it will give leaders the tools and techniques to empower corporate leadership that can change the future of humankind.

Earth is a place where every species should thrive. It's an incredible place, and we are meant to be well – and with, ethics, morality and practice we shall.

CHAPTER 1: WHAT IS THIS EXPERIMENT?

"No matter where you are in your journey, stop and look around. Reflect. This time next year, nothing will be the same." – Mandy Antoniacci

Who was it that suggested that we should never waste a good crisis? When we got together to write this book, we were in the middle of a crisis. Society was at odds with government and business. Nations were at odds with each other. There was a growing polarization of society - and an increase in nationalism fueled by partisan politics and media.

At the same time, we were suffering a significant systemic change in our climate as a result of an uncontrolled use of fossil fuels, unabated population growth that gave rise to modern manufacturing. Through all of this, we saw an exponential increase in inequality.

And then on top of that came an even bigger crisis: Coronavirus disease (COVID-19). Every single one of us was affected in some way. There will be many books written about COVID-19. ***This isn't one of them.***

It is about another pandemic, and it offers a remedy. It's hard to avoid clichés such as – "we're all connected" and "we've never had better access to information" – but these are double-edged if we aren't able to counter any adverse effects. Those responsible for how our societies operate have a new responsibility. Between us, we must think more conscientiously and far more long term.

Our world has become a very different place as we have evolved and quite dangerously a result of recent political history. We need divergent thinking, more ingenuity and considerably better leadership if we are to sustain ourselves in the future.

THE PANDEMIC OF MARKETING

The noise from marketing consumes our society. This noise is in a constant battle for our attention. We are now discovering many mind-bending statistics about the effects of social media on our lives. Social Media is described every day as both "how" and "why" we are infected.

Society has long been fed a diet of misinformation, saturation, and in many cases, overcomplicated information. It's increasingly difficult to avoid the cacophony of criticism. Almost everyone we speak to describes the irritating and irrelevant "marketing" stuff that wasn't asked for and served only to condemn the brand.

Far too often, marketing has been the label given to those in that "department" in effect separated from the business. That has partitioned the expertise so that it's out of reach. Consequently, this has reduced its chance of generating the value that it should. This kind of thinking creates a dangerous boundary. It puts up a wall.

We see the advertising industry decimated. Many commentators suggest it is now all but devoid of the creativity that once caused the sector to shine. The creativity used to have forced creatives to find work in other industries.

Many more businesses are starting to appreciate how each individual is a human being. They are beginning to see the value of considering people as an opportunity for collaboration and value exchange rather than a dollar sign, a number, or a cog in a corporate wheel.

Together, consumers (all of us) have the power to overcome the negative impacts of the pandemic of marketing by voting no to what we don't want. This reality is at the core of how wholesale change can happen. Can you imagine the collective bargaining power of the consumer together with the commercial might of all business (and the attendant supply chains) being shifted by such a sea-change in business ethics?

Collectively, commercial enterprises have more power than governments. Media owners and marketers have a responsibility to both the businesses who need them and the consumers who consume them. Government stands by and may attempt to remain politically correct but will support a productive economy every time.

Whether consumers realize it or not - they have the power - to vote "yes" or "no" to all of it. Unfortunately, it's not often that everyone comes together in a movement to make a mass change. And imagine if they (we) were persuaded more often as a force for good. Suppose more and more conscientious business leaders with the gift of ethical marketing used that power more often.

It does happen sometimes; but, it's infrequent compared to the extent of change the world needs.

Collectively, and individually, businesses have more power than national governments if they have the will and passion. But beyond that, they will require enlightened leadership. Companies can reshape our lives in profound ways without passing laws or holding elections. The big question is, will they?

Marketing is that last mile. Marketing is the short distance between the product of business and our attention. Good marketing and leadership have become the same thing - indistinguishable and synonymous in the digital era. The combination of leadership and marketing is what we've chosen to call the leadership singularity.

Imagine enough of this singularity of thought and will in enough purpose-filled leaders. Imagine this power in the right hands. Imagine that power with the right heart and mind. Imagine that power put to positive use and not used to weaponize hatred or promote selfish gain.

WHY ANOTHER BOOK?

In the past, we might have written a business book restricted to the straightforward subject of effective professional practices. Today, a relevant business book must address a more extensive scope and solve the real challenges for which Marketing was born.

The challenge - and increasingly, the opportunity - for business is how to connect big ideas to everyday actions. And in this new world, how to alter beyond recognition the "why" and "how" with the latest science and technology available.

We believe that the immense global problems we face may only be possible for socially responsible businesses to address. They have the power to address these issues directly at their source by thinking and working differently and at the scale of everyday and individual decisions.

Businesses must work hard to overcome massive barriers that have built up. The words on everyone involved with the strategy's lips is trust. Lousy marketing has destroyed trust for both customers and workforces.

One of the most significant barriers to success is the leaders themselves and the hardest change of all the shift in their mindsets - the attitudes and mentalities, models and ambitions that got us here in the first place.

This book describes a grand vision of what Marketing and business can be and illustrates what these visions could look like in action. It's a wake-up call that Marketing and leadership practices are inextricably linked and critical if the world is to make progress and provide a long-term future for our species.

Based on decades of collective experience, we have written this book in plain language, and we hope it's widely accessible. Our goal is to give hope, insight and guidance for today's leaders - those who want to "market" well and really "lead" in the modern era.

Like never before we see the need to redefine "marketing". It is now, quite literally, a matter of life and death. We've operated for far too long without establishing what a more relevant concept of marketing should be today; and more importantly, how it should be defined for the future.

This book is about how marketing leadership can change the world for the better. Marketing controls the world. **Only marketing can save it**.

CHAPTER 2: WHO IS THE ENEMY?

WHO DID THIS TO US?

That's the typical human response when things are going badly to ask, *"Who did this to us?"*

During the twentieth century, it became abundantly clear that things had gone badly wrong. We needed to know how we ended up here before exploring possible solutions.

Everything was going well. We were in total control. The data showed us progress:

The world is <u>healthier now</u> than in 1800, when 40% of infants died before reaching the age of five. Now, that number is around 10% and declining.

The world is more <u>economically fair</u> compared to just 200 years ago when 85% of the world population lived in extreme poverty. Twenty years ago it was 29%. Today only 9% live in extreme poverty while the majority of people (75%) around the globe live in middle-income countries.

The world is more <u>literate</u> now; and over the last two centuries, literacy rates have spread from a group of wealthy elite citizens to a reality where eight out of 10 people can read.

In the US, for example, 2019 was a thriving year for Americans. The <u>unemployment</u> rate had been at 4% or less for 16 consecutive months, the longest streak in 50 years and jobs grew for 106 straight months, also the longest streak on record.

We were on top of the world. With only two days for a product to be distributed worldwide, we had become *"fast, efficient, and futuristic"*. Yet somehow undetected, a self-perpetuating cycle of greed and consumerism was spreading a human behavior pandemic of its own.

We've watched helplessly as business best practice – trust, creativity, personal development, achievement, marketing, and leadership; all fell by the wayside.

Sadly, the year 2020 has provided humanity with an ironic vision built out of pure hindsight. To the world's chagrin, it has become apparent that the foundation of our situation is very much not under control. What accounts for our failure to translate these concerns into corrective actions? What did we miss, and how could we have got it so wrong?

Marketers and Leaders alike are the frontline practitioners of their trade. They are in the battle for dominance of their markets. They currently exist within an influencer-driven, celebrity fueled capitalistic construct.

Marketers and leaders have been facing off against the following six familiar enemies for years.

ENEMY #1: DATA
We have an unacceptable lack of intangible data.
Historically, marketing has found it quite challenging to evidence its value. In other words, by lacking data and information to establish its position, marketing has been lacking the ability to make its case for delivering value across the organization. But today, marketing is driven by data and backed by research and customer information captured at every stage in the buying process. Deploying techniques that can assess social and behavioral

consumerism leads to smarter tactics. In some cases, the leaders of marketing teams find themselves tempted to tap into addictive strategies.

Without getting too technical, they are using "prefrontal cortex" manipulations that urge the masses to consume – rather than the more subtle, yet thoughtful approaches of integrating coherently into what constitutes "real" value to the customer.

Yet even with all these sophisticated tools, many marketers struggle with the amount of data at their disposal. These are the real-time insights they can access. What's more alarming is that as useful customer information slips through the fingers of marketing leaders, there's a growing movement to restrict corporation's use of the data from the customer end due to the loss of trust.

This lack was painfully evident in Edelman's 17th annual trust and credibility survey, which found that only "52% of respondents to our survey said they trust business to do what is right".

How can corporations even begin to effectively service customer needs, when this is the starting point? The response metrics are even worse.

By way of illustration:

- Only a fraction of firms can react to online customer interactions immediately – (SiteCore)

- 43% of the reactions happen in the pre-purchase stage, 38% during purchase, and just 35% post-purchase
- 31% of the firms lacked in-house skills necessary to analyze the data and just 12% have data at an individual customer level (vs segment or demographic group)
- 65% of brand respondents' organizations are using digital analytics software, with only 30% planning to adopt it

Still to this day, even in digitally savvy organizations, marketing is stigmatized with the incapacity to provide data, for what is conveniently called "intangible" data.

For example:
- How can you measure the level of trust you apply to a brand when you're walking through a supermarket?
- How do you calculate the causal familiarity that will compel you to put a product in your shopping cart?

Unless marketers can reach a statistically significant correlation through, for example - leveraging an Internet of Things (IoT) strategy, they will not have a full framework for consumer behavior. If this remains the case, we may never be able to capture that information outside of controlled online shopping funnels. Even then, do we know the psychological data to inform brand loyalty, or have we simply conditioned consumer behaviors conveniently and predictably?

ENEMY #2: SYSTEMS

Our systems are rigged.

Business processes, systems, and procedures are (in many cases) hard coded in the handbook for how an organization works. They are typically designed/engineered by an extensive external consulting practice complete with all kinds of reporting, measurement, and monitoring techniques and capabilities (if they've been compensated appropriately to do so).

Those processes dictate how departments report their functional activity. Once those systems have been established, it becomes difficult for anything other than the prescribed procedures to be changed.

Marketing is now having to report to the Sales and Finance departments in a way which makes Marketing impossible to report on because the system doesn't allow it.

These systems are designed for the primary benefactor – the organization – not the customer.

As an example: a large national bank in the US is trying to offer new financial services in a very competitive market fixed by core banking processes. In the banking processes, only partial customer data transactions are captured. These data go to external third parties who own the data because that process is hosted outside the enterprise.

The bank has, therefore, lost the crucial transaction data of their customers. The business is now unable to understand the behaviors of the customer journey as it goes through the bank processes. As a result, the Marketing department can't even send an email (or surface mail) to its customers without frustrating and confusing them, because the customer may well have already bought that product from the bank.

To change that system would cost millions. The system is not designed from a customer standpoint, but rather for the customer benefits, and that's true for far too many companies and industries.

Systems are our enemies because they have been allowed to grow weeds, and to create expectations and definitions that are inappropriate and no longer valid as the digital world has transformed the way customers think.

They are designed to move and analyze data at speeds that often hurt their intended purpose. Moreover, they are not able to accurately include weighted metrics to explain the emotional psychology of the customer experience outside of a number scale or emojis without violating some element of needed privacy for the customer.

If the marketing department can't provide the value proposition of needing that data, that core banking system won't change. The challenge, therefore, is to raise the consciousness and enlightenment of the executive leadership to alter their mindset in a sufficient enough way for them to make more intelligent investments.

ENEMY #3: ORGANIZATIONAL DESIGN

Our organizational DNA design is broken.

Back in the days when America started to make railroads, the organizational chart was a pyramid, with one guy at the top, and there was delegation, delegation, delegation and more delegation. There was also a pension and expectation of lifelong employment that was rigorously aligned with the coal mine working hours of 9 am to 5 pm.

According to the Dunbar Number, you can't have more than 150 people in your corporate sphere of responsibility because beyond that; one can't cope with the number of connections. Thus, to go above 150 people leads to breaking down a structure into various subdivisions with their leadership, subculture, governance, language, data, and information.

In the digital world, every cross-functional system or process works to ensure interdependence across the organization, which is why transformation is so hard.

To simplify – let's imagine marketing and leadership jointly as the brains of a "corporate body." Now imagine if they could not appropriately identify, communicate, and simultaneously direct the body with efficiency towards a goal. What happens under these conditions is total anarchy and usually results in the downfall of that corporation. We want to avoid these common shortcomings, but how?

The reality we are facing now is from the damage done over decades of business practices that harden cultural flexibility. When organizational cultures are stuck in the past, they resort to unethical means to remain unaltered. Call it irresponsible, lazy, or immoral leadership – it's clear from examples like the Wells Fargo scandal, that outdated governance and cultural norms contributed to extensive corporate greed. Add to that the predatorial customer practices and hundreds of millions in legal fines from the US government and private citizens. While the company has survived from a business perspective, their trust and reputational prowess have tanked.

This undercurrent of organizational malfeasance is an untenable lack of self-awareness, hidden from leadership, and cloaked in contextless bureaucracy. Business practices like "foursquare" quadrant diagrams and SWOT analyses put everything into neat little and often meaningless boxes to satisfy an attempt at organization excellence. Yet, they will fail due to lack of application. Humans don't operate like that, and when they're forced to collaborate in the context of an organizational construct, acting as a leading entity is a failing issue because marketing is now indivisible from manufacturing.

ENEMY #4: KNOWLEDGE

Knowledge is the real culprit.

What we **know** is based on what we **knew**. That was possibly fine then, but what about now when so much has changed? The context changed so does the reality of what we now know.

Knowledge tends to get in the way. Knowledge emerges through repetitive behaviors fueled by our own experiences and education. Most educated leaders think of marketing as science when the practice is, in fact, closer to art (creativity). MBAs are taught a definition of marketing, which bears no resemblance to the reality of what's needed to do the job.

Most concerningly, even fewer MBA programs include discussions around the importance and application of ethical leadership. Why is that?

Is it because our conditioned corporate ethos has roots in overcoming the odds; thus, it ignores the necessity for risk analysis? Are we afraid to learn that our current value system for business behavior is outdated?

Are we scared to admit that we're simply "no longer with the times" – especially now as it relates to the increased global focus on individual consumerism?

Whatever lagging indicator we think we've captured, one thing's for sure – it's no longer working, and our rate of failure is significantly outpacing our rate of relevant education. What we knew isn't helping any of us.

Is it possible to capture actionable data at the enterprise level that is intelligent and simultaneously aligns with marketing and leadership objectives? What knowledge system have you encountered that can effectively deconflict a set of constantly changing priorities to respond in real-time to a global customer and environmental needs?

Not many come to mind, right? So now take that practical and obvious concern, and then overlay that these systems usually take at least eight months to influence fully – not to mention the internal resources needed to maintain effectively. This rigid, obtuse, and heavy systems-based approach does not encourage the creative capability necessary to syphon real-time data and quickly solve customer concerns – for right now.

Our concern is apparent – our limited knowledge is based on our fixed beliefs, and that prevents us from being creative in a complex world. Whether we call that complacency or enlightenment, somewhere between the two lies our ability as individuals to accept that we know nothing and therefore must start fresh every day to create responsively.

ENEMY #5: MEANING

Overcoming the age of meaningless.

Our definition of meaning is the sense of something. What is meant or intended? It is the conscious, unconscious, and possibly biased intent behind how we align ourselves and influence others. It's this significance that drives performance. It is also at the core of whatever we're trying to get across to others – to market.

History has taught us as a society that we're capable of making a massive impact if we can convey the right meaning. This impact can be either good or bad, but it's still very dependent on the application. Several key factors influence meaning and why we find them to be problematic.

A false meaning will emerge from a corrupted system. And it will be a force to be reckoned with.

Capitalism is predicated on profits. That's the context in which marketing and leadership models have to operate. The motivations for marketing are almost always to drive sales and reputation, which, in turn, drives more sales. All of this creates a profit-based motive and outcome to deliver a return-on-investment (ROI) for shareholders.

In many cases, this sales machine is guided by false or outdated information. As a society, we love to caution against those curious enough to learn "how the sausage gets made," but maybe this old idiom tried to warn us all along. We've seen many organizational studies expose how the current system isn't working for those who make it possible. These fissures from within, always find a way to break confidence in the customer experience, which in turn further damages the corporation's ability to establish and market sustainable meaning.

Meaning comes from definition within a context. When the context is a system that values shareholders more than people, marketing and leadership are governed by decisions predicated on profit. When the system is no longer driving sustainable results for the people, and the planet, it becomes ineffective and corrupt.

Take, for example, the case of WeWork and their recently disenfranchised founder Adam Neumann. The coworking giant created a deceivingly outsized expectation that its definition for the future of work should be rooted in a specific cultural and operational model. As it turns out, the context in which they created this definition was a poisonously self-serving agenda that manipulated EBITDA, investors, and customers.

Billions of investment dollars were dumped into the idea that somehow their proposal would provide for a sustainable practice. Yet, everything crashed down after Neumann was forced to reveal the unethical underbelly of WeWork's operation that didn't align with their lofty goals of establishing credibility as a workplace of higher purpose.

The context WeWork attempted to create, was based on a false pretense. The subsequent damage has been significant. Competitors have swooped in to take workshare as lawsuits, infighting, and cultural confusion indicators have all validated - that meaning without a contextual alignment is quite merely, meaningless.

If marketing is no longer the growth engine, what is its purpose? Should the core value of marketing be in the context of enlightened leadership – the definition of its practical utility must be to weaponize marketing for good – to support businesses role as purpose-driven and accountable leader.

Therefore, a new meaning would arise for a CEO as being purposeful for whom the standard definition of a purposeful goal creates the purpose-driven organization.

In essence, it doesn't matter what we believe the definition of marketing to be because everyone will have their interpretation. It is, however, the responsibility of marketers or leaders to redefine and rethink the meaning of marketing in our new context.

ENEMY #6: GAMING

We've gamed the system.

Gaming the system is manipulating the rules designed to govern an economic ecosystem to gain an advantage over other users, and it has become a widespread practice. It's resulted in a culture that can freely accept known lies, diversionary strategies, misinformation, gaslighting - this pandemic has many names. It breeds a society of stupidity.

As an example, in marketing, black hat SEO methods, such as keyword stuffing, are an attempt to game the search engine's system for ranking websites. Similarly, the actions of patent trolls are an attempt to game the system established to protect the rights of legitimate patent holders.

In the operational structures discussed earlier with divisions, each manager games the system for their ends. With such different attitudes, the leadership at the top of the company can be completely innocent about what's going on inside the organization.

A few years ago, we worked with a pharmaceutical drug company launching a new drug for schizophrenia. What causes schizophrenia is an imbalance in dopamine which goes through our central nervous system and runs up the back of our neck into our brain. Schizophrenia results in individuals losing touch with reality. The same is true of smokers. People who smoke have similar characteristics common to schizophrenia because half of their brain is telling them that it's okay.

Every habit or addiction we have, whether it's obesity, smoking, or alcoholism is caused by a more or less mild form of schizophrenia. So when the company decided to do both, sell digital cigarettes and the drug that can solve the addiction, for some reason, somewhere in that organization, someone had persuaded themselves that was a right decision based on an irrefutable and undeniable alternate schizophrenia, and that is gaming the system.

Today, many unsatisfied and realistic leaders and marketers are looking for a new game. A game that would allow each of us to start our day by bringing our experiences, making new judgments (without being prejudicial to or ignoring what needs to be done), and result in inappropriate decisions.

This new game is a journey of making decision quality and finding a way to be authentic with the system with values that are beneficial for profits, people, and the planet.

From our traditional leadership model – of a few individuals at the top "feeding" the people – is emerging a new way where everyone is empowered and motivated to do the right thing, more often than the wrong thing.

A FINAL THOUGHT

The six enemies of marketing are, in effect, nested like Russian dolls.

The "enemies" we broke apart above are deeply interconnected and entangled. Each enemy was made more potent by reliance on the other. Understanding this interconnection, we can design a different future.

- By understanding data correctly, we can develop more appropriate systems.

- Armed with systems that use data for more valuable outcomes, we can create and empower more purposeful organizations.

- Organizations that are this dynamic will ensure sound knowledge of a more real-time nature that solves for today's not yesterday's challenges.

- The meaning that emerges will be more compelling and valid and significantly remove the need for harmful and corrosive gaming of the system in the first place.

CHAPTER 3: WHAT BROUGHT US HERE?

Leadership and Marketing in the Age of the Pilotless Plane

WHO'S FLYING THIS THING ANYWAY?

Have you ever woken up from a nap, to hear that lovely message: *"please put your tray tables away and your seats in their full upright position, we've begun our descent, and we'll be landing shortly"*?

It's a great feeling, isn't it? You've been delivered to a destination unconsciously, without a single worry. The question is, did you land at your desired destination? If not, you're looking for the first place to air that grievance as you solemnly swear to never fly with that airline again. Frustrating is hardly the word, right?

As leaders of the plane, pilots know that diverting a flight plan can have a dramatic impact on the passengers and crew. Those along for the ride have no control over the flight decisions or external conditions. You bought a ticket knowing full well that plans were *"subject to change"* (your baggage may end up in Bermuda as well).

That's where we are today with Leadership and Marketing. We've committed tremendous resources, infrastructure, and brainpower building the internet – humanity's most highly coveted method for transporting new business objectives. The ecosystem expanded, modified, and commercialized to a predictive degree that has seamlessly prescribed our human behavior right into the caring hands of those in charge.

The robots gave us wings, but will they buckle our seatbelts in turbulence? Vast swaths of consumers have been packaged, virtually assigned a seat, autonomously loaded on planes through predictive funnels, moved through cyberspace with behavioral models, artificial intelligence (AI), and avatars. How fast you walk, what vehicle you're in, your search preferences and connections are collated before you even arrive at the gate. We enjoyed this early on; we felt the warm embrace of systems that seemingly knew what we wanted at every turn.

Was Coronavirus the flight detour we desperately needed? We thought that building automation into every aspect of our lives would save us time, money, and pain in every way. Sure life has picked up speed, but was that really "*a want*", or did we mistakenly program it into humanity as "*a need*"?

Is this the point where we lost cabin pressure? Maybe this was the litmus test of the automated system. It failed to get to the heart of the issue. When the robotic receptionist treated us wrong, we cried out for a human to fix the problem. We found ourselves obsessively pressing "0" until we got a customer service representative. There's something instinctual about exclusively entrusting other bipedal homo sapiens to not only field our problem but also help us resolve how we feel. So until AI can reproduce humanity without our input, we're going to need human leaders to help us navigate through it.

Economists eager to calm jittery nerves have advised us that the economy is certainly not heading into a second Great Depression as a result of the COVID-19 crisis. The distinction, they tell us, is that while there were fundamental structural problems with the financial system for at least a decade before the Wall Street crash of 1929, there are no such structural problems in the economy today. The fundamentals of the economy are healthy, they say, noting that before the arrival of the coronavirus, we had enjoyed 11 straight years of growth, the longest bull market in history.

Such advice, along with substantial financial generosity from government agencies, has been sufficient to soothe the stock market. Nonetheless, within this reassurance itself is hidden the fundamental structural problem that poses the greatest threat to the economy. When economists say that "*we*" have enjoyed the longest bull market in history, they are describing people like themselves. For many others, the last decade has been characterized by economic stagnation or even recession.

Enter the leaders, marketers and mavens of modern information. The people who are in charge are the ones who influence what the masses consume across the nation. Humans are resistant to change, as our evolutionary code favors stability and safety. Indeed the lifeforce inside each of us wants to expand and grow – but without having other humans to share in that expansion - are we going where we really want to go? Or are we only mindlessly responding to an automated demand that is spinning our mental wheels in the sand?

Reverting to the time before the virus, we noticed something missing. We asked why our leaders are turning over in record numbers at our corporations. We were sick of misinformation, unsourced, unscientific, biased, and baseless as it all was. We missed looking into the eyes of someone – to test the empirically intangible emotional intelligence quotients – a skill we spent millions of years refining in evolution.

Our trust grew weary, our patience thin. We made promises that we would never work for poor leadership again. Many resorted to self-employment, rather than expose themselves to a scenario that only would annoy them.

According to the Pew Research Center, even in the United States where the social safety net is thin and private investment is more prevalent than in many other countries, only 52 percent of families own any stock at all. What's more, most of the families that own stock have small portfolios – a median of $40,000 in the entire U.S. population, and a median of only $26,000 in stock among middle-class households with annual income of between $53,000 and $100,000. Most stock is held by the wealthy. The 1 percent most wealthy American families own 50 percent of stocks. The top 10 per cent owns 84 percent of the available stocks.

For most people, financial investments are a minor part of the economy. They get by on their wages, rather than on dividends. Wages, unlike the stock market, failed to grow at all for the decade after the end of the 2008 recession. Only in 2019 did wages begin to rise.

Alas, can we put all the blame on leaders? Did they not see

this coming? Did they not care to put the human at the center of our fresh and sexy software code?

Then, the unthinkable happened.

A vicious worldwide virus made us shelter in place, separating humanity from in-person interactions, and connecting us only through cyberspace. Ironic that we had all the tools we thought we needed in spades, but in reality, all we really needed was to see another human face.

We lost the pilot, don't trust the robot, and now every piece of crucial information seems increasingly less credible than we ever could have thought.

Within one month, a quarter of the U.S. population was thrown out of work. As a result of prolonged wage stagnation, many ran out of savings within just a few weeks. In March of 2020, one-third of American families could not pay their rent. Because of a lack of investment in strong healthcare infrastructure, the United States suffered the greatest shock of the COVID-19 crisis so far.

Of course, the problem isn't restricted to Americans. Just as the virus has spread around the world, so has the economic impact. Just as working Americans have taken the brunt of the blow, the uninvested majority of the global population is dealing with trouble that the investors of the world don't have to cope with.

Even as news of this economic suffering spread, stock markets rebounded. The economy of the fortunate has remained fortunate. For the rest, depression looms large.

Inequality is the fundamental structural problem in the economy that economists have been unable or unwilling to see. Behind this economic inequality, however, rests an even more troubling social division, a gap that has made the blindness to inequality possible. The growing distance between investors and workers reflects a larger estrangement in commercial culture: a chasm between the machinery of financial productivity and the human beings who live and work in the economy.

The severe method of social distancing that has characterized the COVID-19 crisis is not a complete departure from previous practice, but a dramatic amplification of what was already taking place.

Was this the moment of truth? When our faith in leadership gave out? When marketing was exposed as manipulation of those with the loudest shout? Time always gives us the power to look in reverse, the sick trick is now all of us are faced with re-evaluating our belief systems before we end up in a hearse. So for now, we'll call this diversion a blessing – for our regularly scheduled human flight path – but, as always only time will tell if it all adds up after we do the math.

Remote work has been expanding since the 1990s. Remote interactions between businesses and their customers have been on the increase as well, as customer service counters gave way to customer service call centers that in turn are being replaced by automated telephone service and chatbots.

This growth of social distancing within business has delivered an undeniable growth in financial efficiency. However, this economic benefit has come at a cost: an impoverishment of the human experience of business.

SHOULD LEADERS AND MARKETERS WEAR THE MASK, A LITTLE BIT LONGER?

Information was lost and manipulated as much as our faith in corporate leadership. We were reaching an iteration where virtual approvals, likes, and follows weren't making us better human fellows. We entered a drift. A minefield of information, apps, and dinner choices that caused a rift. In the same room, but miles apart, we failed to blend the advantages of technology into the human heart.

Traditional leadership models built pyramids, promoted pensions, and put people last far too often. Toxicity in the workplace has skyrocketed at a record rate, even at corporations that we once considered to be great. Whether exposed online or sued until they ran out of money and time - the once covetously secure position of leadership is now more endangered than a tiger at Joe Exotic's Zoo.

Without the human connection that was once at the core of business, trust in brands has withered. The pervasive automation of marketing has led most brands to become mere commodities. The result is a business landscape populated by vast monocultures where once diverse economic ecosystems thrived.

The machine learning that powers business today, both depends upon, and delivers predictability. When times are good, the yield is remarkable. However, as with all monocultures, the system has grown vulnerable to rapid disruption when pestilence arrives.

But wait, there's more.

What was once our primary information system commonly found as a staple on the kitchen table, turned into 140 characters and an emoji of what you see on the barn floor of a stable. Left to our own devices, the masses consumed everything about humanity that we can clearly classify as mindless vices.

The leader's role was becoming less and less critical, and trust was about as reliable as finding treasure in a "Goonies" pirate chest. To simply observe, we got here by going nowhere fast and when Coronavirus came along – it exposed just how long we allowed this mindless, heartless, and leaderless way to last. **If we remove the pilot, let's see how far we can really fly.**

CHAPTER 4: WHAT ARE THE NEW IDEAS?

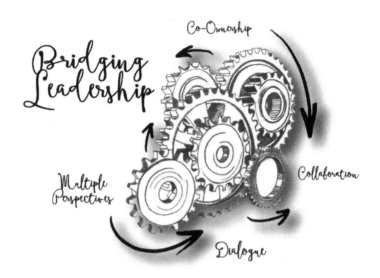

"Sometimes, problems don't require a solution to solve them; Instead, they require maturity to outgrow them." – Steve Maraboli

THE RISE OF THE NEW MARKETER

Marketing has to mature. It can no longer be a bolt on to the business to help sell the product to an unsuspecting customer base – it needs to be built-in.

Marketing must be inseparable from everything in the business. And everyone in the company has to think about marketing. It must be interwoven with everything the business stands for.

In an increasingly automated world, marketing is the definition of the business. Think of the companies that are so automated (digitalized) that the products rarely see human intervention.

Think about that. Warehouses now filled with robots making cars and everything that used to be assembled by humans. Think of the new banking systems and businesses that are almost entirely automated – fintech.

Every industry on Earth is now becoming a software business to some degree. We are not saying that's the future for everything – the removal of all humans in favor of that science fiction dystopia – but it should certainly raise the importance of how we connect our business with our customers.

Maturity is not for everyone.
It's for the conscientious individual and conscious leaders. Especially those leaders that have the mindset that the world needs to be sustainable. Maturity means that we've learned and have done the math that shows how humanity needs to change and that the business has a role in that.

Maturity is a leadership attitude that demands that we stand up to the system that would crush us because of its selfish inequity and inequality - this is hard. Marketing and leadership must become indivisible. The administration of the business must recognize that marketing is not a department; it is the business. The idea of marketing in the digital era has to be completely redefined.

THE NEW MARKETER/LEADER

The Three M's.

1. **Marketing is the mechanism** by which a business makes promises to its audiences. Marketing creates the story and develops the meaning that it takes to the consumers and beneficiaries. It describes the enterprise and what it can do its customers.

2. **Manufacturing is the mechanism** through which the business makes the stuff that's promised. This can be service, solution, or product. The company either does the "making" itself or oversees the process and increasingly has to understand how that looks and feels in the market.

3. **Management is the leadership**, the strategic path, the vision and administration of it all - the oversight and execution of the business. In the digital era, this includes marketing that's interwoven with the manufacturing processes. It's the work of everyone within an organization to

efficiently and effectively coordinate and connect the methods and systems that comprise #1 and #2.

What else is there?

This new maturity of marketing is real leadership. The modern leader/marketer has a responsibility to stop the business thinking of these labels as in some way divided. The future demands marketing leaders to be business leaders who can see how inextricable these concepts are.

It won't be a marketing question, but it will be a marketing leadership answer. Digitalization won't stop, and neither must the lazy adherence to how things once were.

The mature leader is the one that has long since recognized the inevitability of this and has already moved to look after their people and infrastructure to prepare them for this new reality.

The mature leader is comfortable with digitalization, uncertainty, and ambiguity. They know that market dynamics and technology together have disrupted everything. These forces have shortened the time and distance between "marketing" and "manufacturing" and the odds of success for anyone misunderstanding that fact.

The promise to the audience is entirely on display to all of us in a digitized business. The audience sees what's made (and what's being made in the future) right there. The promise is palpable, viewable, experienceable and comparable in every dimension. In every sense. All the time. And especially when it fails. What manufacturing does is now what marketing is.

CONDITIONS FOR THE NEW BUSINESS OF MARKETING

The six dimensions of maturity we need for the future:

Dimension #1: The Art of Imagination and Insight

To get to the future, first, we need to use our heads. This new world demands that we go beyond the normal and that tired definition of creativity and tick the box called imagination. We have to get way beyond the standard cursory considerations of what gets classified as creativity.

Imagination in this new world means we have to transcend anything superficial when planning the roadmap to the future. It means doing the hard work to get inside the minds of today's customers – finding the real insight* and as a result redesigning everything to get there.

Such insight means being able to identify and understand something so clearly and uniquely that you can make a decision that will make a positive difference.

That takes imagination and a significant shift of effort.

Dimension #2: That Elusive Objectivity

Leadership is often described as a lonely place. The mature marketing leader needs objectivity like never before; but, where will it come from? It's impossible to be objective about yourself.

It's no use getting objective advice from those with a vested interest such as the consultancies and marketing agencies who will have to win back their trust. Leaders make hard decisions, and now, many more of them that are unlikely to be welcomed.

Objective challenge of an impartial nature is physically impossible within the constructs of a single business. As a mature leader, it's essential to get that check and balance, so finding that trusted source of objectivity is paramount.

Developing the correct standard of objectivity means having the infrastructure in place that enables testing and allows for a challenge. It must be done with integrity to avoid comfortable/traditional thinking. The aim is to get to the truth where everyone is alive to the reality.

Dimension #3: The Courage to Change

When it comes to planning for the new market future, every business is on the edge of a precipice. It is a leap into the dark, and it's going to take brave leaders to build new visions. In a world of uncertainty, not one of us is fully prepared for what is to come. The years we've spent and the lessons we've learned getting here is no guarantee that we are equipped to handle what's to come. Knowledge is not a basis for the right decisions any longer – it may even be a real risk.

How willing we are to accept that we don't know what's required or how to change are perhaps the biggest questions of all. And then having the courage and resilience to back up the decisions we have made. We have to upgrade what gives us our courage. Going in a direction for the first time, saying yes when the outcome is unclear but needs to be proven, asking the difficult questions that challenge long-held assumptions – all takes courage.

Where that courage comes from requires work. It rests on you knowing yourself and your capabilities well. It requires you to be sure that your decisions come from a place of purity, morality, and reason. This is a place where you can look back and be happy with your position even if it proves to be wrong.

Dimension #4: The Shift in Investment

If choices made regarding investment don't support the new visions we create, then the business will not *"get there"*. And we don't just mean cash.

Real investment and commitment are required in resources, time and energy, refocusing people's attention on the new purpose and vision.

Senior executives – now more than ever – need to engage with big ideas and in different markets.

If new decisions don't result in the *"irrevocable allocation"* of resources, then it isn't a real decision. And if that's the case, then no investment has been made.

The business will never get to the new *"there"*.

Dimension #5: The All-Critical Alignment

The mature marketer must be expert collaborators. A group of individuals taken together is called a collective. The business of marketing needs to create a collective sense of purpose – the concepts of unification, coherence, combined intelligence, and optimization (effectiveness and efficiency).

Alignment and coherence can only be achieved through collaboration and integrated action. It has become a baseline for good practice as businesses seek to exploit every weapon available to bring about effective and smart outcomes.

Dimension #6: Execution, Execution, Execution

It's a fact that strategy is irrelevant without execution. No amount of great thinking will achieve your desired future or outcome. You need to make real change in the practical sense. Acting differently makes others think and work differently.

It may sound obvious, but many businesses cannot implement practical steps.

REDEFINING MARKETING

"Problems are nothing but wake-up calls for creativity." – Gerhard Gschwandtner

Marketing Singularity

The term singularity describes the moment when a system changes so much that its rules and technologies are incomprehensible to previous generations. Think of it as a point-of-no-return in history.

It calls for a new standard of creativity and leadership. To us, Marketing now stands at the forefront of this new era. Dramatic changes and advances in consumer expectation, purchasing habits, greater acceptance and use of modern technology – it all means the ways we've thought and worked in the past are now in constant flux.

The singularity completely redefines everything that's gone before and creates the need for a new language and definition of marketing leadership.

The Reality of Digitalization

Automating core business processes and systems to increase efficiency and effectiveness is now long underway in most businesses. Businesses are getting used to techniques and technology, often third parties (systems, software and hardware, transformation consultants, culture change experts) and deploying resources to transform existing business processes.

Businesses are installing complete platforms and solutions for increased customer experience, business performance, and all the transactions and actions within. It forces the marketing professional to be more thoughtful than ever before. We can see already how insensitive and dismissive these systems can be.

AI is causing a new ethical dilemma; there are new forms of "have" and "have not". There are many more people disenfranchised and abused by the phenomena of digitalization of everything.

The new marketer has a massive responsibility. Everything that's heard seen and sensed from a given brand enterprise or utility is part of the promise a business can make. If the product or solution has integrity and purpose – something that is ethically and morally valuable – it has a new-found opportunity to present new value and deliver an authentic story of the future business to a more welcoming audience.

The totality of this gets called a wide range of things: brand, awareness, experience, and reputation. It is the new and evolving componentry that adds up to the favorable choice – one solution over another. The modern marketer has a weapon for good or evil at their disposal. History will be the judge as to what side the marketer chooses to come down on.

A NEW DEFINITION OF MARKETING

To establish and deploy the purpose in the last mile – a mission that's filled with meaning and relevance for chosen audiences. It recognizes ethics and a kind of morality that seeks to serve society, the people that work for the firm, and the community. It involves helping the planet and the nature that we thrive within. It is no longer just about making money for invisible shareholders.

It involves bringing a level of mastery of (at least) the following:

- **The Journey** – Establishing the vision and direction of everything the business does.
- **The Plan** – Creating the strategy and plan that can take the whole business (departments, teams, divisions, sectors)
- **The Intelligence** – Knowing data and their whereabouts. What condition it is in, who owns it

inside or outside the traditional definition of a business.

- **The Forensics** – The insights exist inside the data. A framework within which that data is interrogated is required so that it gives up these insights in pursuit of a vision.
- **Market Awareness** – A robust appreciation of the chosen audiences. It involves knowing who our consumers are - their needs, wants, hopes and aspirations.
- **Brand Mastery** – Creating the brand (i.e., going way beyond the logo) means establishing the promise and proposition - it embraces the advertising - on and offline - and the traditional definition of marketing deliverables - collateral.
- **Media Mastery** – It demands knowing how media planning and buying happens and operates in this digital era.
- **Reputation Mastery** – Knowing how to design the PR strategy and manage the content and narratives that sit within it - the messaging, value propositions, the story
- **Positioning** – Establishing what the corporate identity needs to be from the packaging of the entire idea (i.e., solutions, products, experience)

through to making tangible the spirit of the business.

- **Digital Savviness** – Developing the User Interfaces (UI) and User Experiences (UX) that consumers see through their devices - given at least 80% of consumers will meet the business there.

- **Curiosity** – Continuously being curious about how things are changing every second of every day – the research and analytics that improve our awareness and gives the course correction – extracted from the insight and data – driving decision making inside the organization.

A NEW DEFINITION OF LEADERSHIP

"Bridging Leadership*" is a style of leadership that's required right now.

It is a new mentality. It rests on some essential skills: listening, empathy, and self-awareness—the ability to connect with different audiences and stakeholders. The bridging leader will be secure in themselves, with low ego needs. A systems thinker with the ability to design, convene and manage a process of partnership.

At the core, the bridging leader can create that safe place for creativity and progress to happen. By creating and sustaining effective working relationships among key partners and stakeholders, resolution and the removal of unnecessary conflict are attained.

By "bridging" the different perspectives and opinions to be found across various stakeholders, a joint plan can be developed and shared to find solutions for business, social and economic problems.

The concept of bridging leadership was developed by an international group of researchers and development practitioners convened by the Synergos Institute in New York over the last 25 years.

Bridging Leadership is an approach to leadership for addressing complex challenges.

These challenges are:
- Typically beyond the capacity of one sector alone to resolve.
- In need of the collaborative action of all sectors – government, civil society, business, and donors.
- In need of sustainable solutions that are owned by diverse and multiple stakeholders.

The Characteristics of Bridging Leaders
- From commander and controller – to facilitator and convener.

- From the sole owner of the problem and solution – to prime mover and co-owner of the problem **and** solution.
- From having all the answers to the creator of the conditions where solutions emerge
- From a single intelligence to a focuser of collective attention. The distiller of collective intelligence.
- From the head of one organization to the ligament between organizations and institutions across a system
- From the holder of the power to the distributor of energy, letting go to enable new things to emerge.
- From expert to a non-expert – mobilizing the expertise of others.

We believe these apply as much to our challenge as marketers of business as they do to social difficulties in the broadest sense.

A NEW DEFINITION OF MANUFACTURING

The "making" (the creation) – a thoughtful, responsible, sustainable, ethical design, and making of the substance, product, service, or solution.

The plant, infrastructure, supply chain, resources, systems, skills, rules, procedures, techniques, and capabilities to make or do what the organization makes/does.

A NEW DEFINITION OF MANAGEMENT

We must always remember that a business is made up of humans. Even if it is increasing applying new technological tools, it's the people that benefit and are involved that are important.

The mature mindset, mentality, and attitude of leaders and the workforce to manage in an ethical, moral and sustainable way. The organizational design, the management, payroll, strategy, and leadership.

The decisions that ensure marketing makes the most efficient and effective interface with manufacturing – and vice versa. Managing the partners – e.g., distribution of what gets made – the substance and so on.

Business is Human After All

The coronavirus crisis has simultaneously revealed the great potential for digital technology to facilitate business interactions over a distance and exposed the limitations of that technology in providing the essential elements of human contact.

We have discovered in a physical world in which our expressions of emotion must always remain masked, that we have:

- A hunger for face-to-face interaction.
- A need for full human connection. That nature of contact that cannot be achieved on screen.
- A feeling of skin hunger. This is the emotion that arises out of deprivation from human touch.

The rediscovery of the vital importance of humanity to business can inspire us to develop techniques of robust emotional experience to match the dominant technologies of digital information now at our fingertips.

A business has the opportunity to synthesize new kinds of platforms that are at once digitally powered and infused with humanity. This new direction for business will be fully embodied, informed by the insight that, after all, human beings are not computers with bodies attached. We're biological, hormonal, muscle, and sinew fully integrated with a neural net.

We are part of a greater whole.

What's more, we have learned through the struggles provoked by COVID-19 that we are more than just individuals. We live and die as communities, flattening the curve of infection, and maintaining public health only when we work together. In this forced experiment, everyone's contribution counts, regardless of income or social status.

In the past, attention in business has focused on executive leadership, because that's where the money is. We see more clearly now that the entire community of a business contributes vitally to its place in society – to achieving its vision and that all involve the new definition of marketing, from the C-suite to the clerks and employees on the front line.

Acceleration

The pace of business has focused on the industrial metaphor of the need for speed. Still, the unanticipated pause created by the coronavirus has forced companies to slow down. And in the process to rediscover the distinct advantages of unhurried moments.

The interlude has led to moments of self-reflection that, though they are often painful in their clarity, are necessary to keep business cultures on a dependable and trustworthy course.

Marketing can no longer remain a superficial gloss on coldly-engineered machinery of profit.

Consider This: the CEOs, who signed a declaration of purpose in 2019 to realign their businesses to benefit shared human values. They have been exposed, by a New York Times investigation. They were maintaining dividend payments and extravagant executive compensation packages even as they fired hundreds of thousands of employees.

Sustainable marketing is impossible when trust has been eroded. When promises are not kept, when actions contradict communications, even the most sincere messaging cannot be accepted at face value.

Just as public health programs require consistent, community-wide action to be maintained, corporate financial health requires that businesses be maintained as entire communities, rather than allowing executive headquarters to attempt to survive while cut free from the body of the company.

To enact this new version of total corporate health, we seek new metrics of overall company fitness to replace the short term, limited metrics. Business requires a new kind of data science and design, one that doesn't aim for the minimally viable product, but maximal viability. Optimization is out, replaced by the enhancement of experiences in the workplace and the marketplace, expanding possibilities rather than narrowing them down to their most directly efficient forms.

In this new environment, we seek technology that plays with us, building in delight in contrast from the digital, rather than the technology that proves its power by defeating humanity in elaborately staged games of chess.

The new goal is to use digital technology to enhance our understanding rather than to detract from it.

Fantasies of a *"Singularity"* that brings about a post-human future are giving way to new visions of a Plurality in which humanity thrives in diverse relationships with its technology.

We've learned the hard way that even the most significant datasets can't bring us complete and entirely accurate predictions of market conditions, even in the near term. Readiness for uncertainty and acceptance of the ambiguity of data must now be integrated as fundamental aspects for models of sustainable marketing.

The first businesses were literal cultures, enterprises of horticulture and agriculture. The enterprises that survived were those that re-invested wealth back into the ground from which it came, rather than hoarding it to the point of artificial scarcity.

As conventional business supply chains fail to provide food security during this crisis, it's time for a return to the idea of running a business as a sustainable ecosystem rather than as an industrial machine. The new goal must not be continual growth, but the acceptance of cycles of death and renewal, flourishing in summer while anticipating and preparing for the winters to come.

The coronavirus crisis is a test of fitness in business, but not in a Darwinian sense of survival of the fittest. The crisis reminds us that no business can live forever, just as no human can avoid death, but only delay it. Reminded of the universality of death, we might also adopt the new business motto: **Memento mori**.

We remember that all our work will eventually perish. Knowing this, we ask ourselves the essential questions: How do we choose to work in the meantime? What kind of business do we want to run while we can? How can we help our clients and customers to live in fulfilment, while they can?

CHAPTER 5: EMERGING STRATEGIES

What strategies are emerging for a New

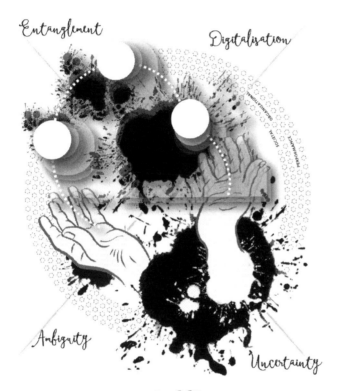

World?

> *"It isn't that they cannot find the solution. It is that they cannot see the problem." – G.K Chesterton*

Before we get into the strategies, let's quickly summarize where we've got to.

The idea of leadership singularity, the theme that drove this book, demands that those in control of the future of their business accept their responsibility to humankind.

However infinitesimally small they feel their business, or niche business is – however hard the challenge will be to shift mindsets and stubborn outdated systems.

The marketing leader is accountable.

1. **Leader** - The role of a leader is to inspire the business, its audiences, systems and workforce through coherent communication of the vision and its plan.
2. **Marketer** - The role of a marketer is to inspire the business, its audiences, systems and workforce through coherent communication of the vision and its plan.

For marketing to mature into leadership, and leaders to mature into marketers – the new leader marketers have responsibility.

- They have to be enlightened – conscious/aware of the threat we face as a society and understand their role in combating the decline in values and trust.

- They have to reunite their communities to create interdependent relationships between all bodies of work within their organization and their broader eco-systems.
- They have to understand the responsibility for societal change and value creation for human beings and the planet.
- They must be comfortable with digitalization, uncertainty, and ambiguity.

In other words, Marketing/Leadership and the singularity we need is when we take the responsibility to change the world in which we live and embody others' interests together with those of the planet upon which we rely merged with regenerative economics.

A PERFECT MOMENT IN TIME

A Mantra of Momentum. These new leaders/marketers will gain courage and experience different energy as change gains momentum. As progress emerges, there will be a shift in behavior, increasing exponentially as a new sense of purpose feeds further investment.

IMAGINE THE NEW WORLD INFORMED BY THE OLD

It seems a little strange to categorize 2005 as being old, but it's a useful frame for the pace of innovation and transformation. It's critical to have it in our minds, though when thinking about developing strategies for the future.

2005

- Facebook was one year old – an American college phenomenon.
- Instagram and WhatsApp were not even twinkles in the eye.
- Skype, started by Estonian entrepreneurs in 2003 didn't add video until 2006.
- Social media wasn't a term anyone would recognize.
- Friends Reunited was bought by ITV (A TV Channel in the United Kingdom) in 2005.
- YouTube was born that same year.

2006

- Twitter was born.

2007

- Apple launched the iPhone.

- That year eight million households had a broadband connection.
- What we called desktop computers had access to the internet at speeds up to 10 megabits per second (Mbps).
- It took a minute and a half to download an album.
- Seven million homes in the UK used dial-up connections.

All of the innovations above started with someone having an idea. To go beyond them is to dream in an uncertain world. This will be the cornerstone for many a future strategy. For us to imagine the new plan, we have to imagine a new world with only one guarantee - nothing is guaranteed.

The marketing leader's role will be to develop their unique formula for turning dreams into ideas into realities, and many of these capabilities are not written on that many CV's.

What follows are a set of conditions - what we might call the Leadership Singularity framework.

A SET OF CONDITIONS

Dream Making

> *"We all have dreams. But to make dreams come into reality, it takes an*

awful lot of determination, dedication, self-discipline, and effort." – Jesse Owens

Dreams are the instigators of our ideas. They have formed the foundation of humanity because the bedrock of our society is our ideas. Without dreams, the marketer would simply be an administrator. Without dreams, the business will remain trapped in the category of commodity.

There are three kinds of marketers:
1. Those that are content to follow the category
2. Those that improve the category
3. Those that invent an entirely new category.

When you think about it, ideas are easy things to have and mostly impossible to deliver. Ideas, like dreams, begin as ghostly concepts. They tend to be elusive, personal, and challenging to define.

Saving the world needs new ideas.
Our world and the humanity it contains have never needed ideas more than it needs them right now. These ideas need to come to life through the strategies and plans that make them real.

We plan that by combining leaders and marketers, they will use their businesses to change the course of humanity and save us from the tyranny of corruption and inequality driven by outdated economic principles that serve a tiny minority to the detriment of everyone else.

Great ideas must survive.

In business, ideas usually come under immediate attack. That's because they signal threat, change, and hard work. So, they need nurturing. They are tough to 'land' in the traditional business context. Existing systems and processes gang up on them and kill them shortly after birth.

It's the job of the marketing leader to change all that. They must get rid of the hecklers, create fertile soil for the roots of the idea to grow, and nurture them until they reach adulthood.

What makes a good idea?

This is a highly contextual question. Bad ideas have made it to market. And terrible ideas can be extremely virulent and endure beyond our wildest imagination (e.g., Al Qaeda, Reality TV, human trafficking, cigarettes, high fructose corn syrup and fast food). These examples would probably be classified as bad ideas to some but not necessarily all those reading this book.

Ideas thrive in the right context.

The ingredients of making a good idea start within the right context. In business, this means understanding the essential dynamics and situations inherent in the market. It means having a set of criteria for what makes anything a success. This demands that the intention, outcome, purpose, objectives, and aims to align with the requirements of every stakeholder.

The idea 'baseline' for the leader marketer:

- **Difference** – It has to be powerfully distinguishable from the competition.
- **Valuable** – It has to be high in utility and appeal.
- **Attention-Grabbing** – It needs an idea with the power to break through the noise.
- **Passionate** – It must inspire passion in those responsible for making it.
- **Timely** – It requires that we find the right moment to make a first impression.
- **Able to Scale** – It must appeal to sufficient numbers of people for it to gather its momentum.
- **Unique** – This one will be rare, but it should be something nobody has dreamed of before.

The future marketer/leader will be a thinker. They will align with the above and be ahead of this. They will know how to translate 'next trends' and apply them to their situation and context.

This is not a new mindset for an existing marketer/leader. It's just not frequent enough. To achieve this level takes ingenuity and demands perpetual curiosity. It's a required attitude to survive in this marketplace. It's desperately needed to win. A healthy mindset for 'now' forces us to think. Imagine what will happen and change if it can harness these new ingredients.

As a result, the business can turn the new thinking and ideas to their advantage and benefit (primarily) the marketplace. At the same time, the leader will have to imagine all the blockers, detractors, challenges, barriers, naysayers, and things that are even more impossible to imagine and remove them before they have a chance to strike.

FUTURE TECHNOLOGY

"The major problems in the world are the result of the difference between how nature works and the way people think" – Gregory Bateson.

Society is at odds with the natural systems, and that's breeding very real-world challenges. Poverty, conflict, famine, the extinction of significant parts of the ecology humans need to exist, the oceans and climate change – we may think they are not part of the brands we create and the commerce that results but we would be fatally mistaken.

Humankind cannot continue to continue with that arrogant and entitled position and expect to survive. The truly great thing is that as new business models emerge, so do the new ways we can support ethical brands to help those in need. The purpose-driven business based on purpose-driven ideas is happening.

There's no shortage of challenges - many of them wicked. There are some signs of hope - several of the largest brands/businesses now have ethical leaders at their helms. Several are turning their attention to the challenge and are attracting backing to fix these issues.

The new technology for social media was heralded as the savior for a long time. It's not been that socially good. And there's been notable failures. The most prominent platforms for hope have become the biggest culprits for despair and need to be held to account. That's a different book.

Artificial intelligence (AI) and machine learning have given us an entirely new toolkit/toybox as marketing leaders. They enable business systems to learn and act intelligently. This phenomenon is already transforming everything around us. To ignore the opportunity to turn this to a decisive advantage in our businesses would be to miss the lifeboat.

The New Work of The Marketing Leader

Many are asking whether technology will replace creativity. We say it can, and in the future, it probably will – but for now, the uniquely human and emotional part of the creative process remains our domain. The co-creativity and augmented design we've shown so far means we will happily coexist – for now.

Technology is a black art for some but the new art form for others. Just consider some of the themes that the competition are using to make a difference in their business. What can we do if we turn these techniques to bigger and better results?

- **The Media Advantage** - Without any human intervention, machines are writing advertisements, creating artwork, and developing designs and placing them on media platforms. How much more can we create?

- **The Immersive Advantage** - We are expanding and extending our realities – virtual reality, augmented reality, and mixed reality – immersive digital experiences with the power to transform healthcare, education and business. What can we envision?

- **Making At A Distance** - 3D and 4D printing - hailed as the heroic warrior during the global health crisis – printing parts that had become unavailable. What more can we do?

- **Connecting Everything** - The Internet of Things (IoT) - the increasing number of 'smart' devices and objects connected to the internet. We talk to inanimate objects answering more correctly by the day. Digital applications – machines are already our secretary – transcribing our meetings and recognizing the different voices. What else should we connect?

- **Experience Everything - Now** - Mass personalization and 'micro-moments' while jargon to most but are essential concepts in the Marketer/Leaders world. We are now acquainted with online personalized shopping experiences. We are quickly becoming blasé about the infinite combinations of everything we command via online shopping. What experience can we create?

- **Calculate Anything** - In the future, the exponential growth of the amount of data will allow the marketing leader to interpret anything/everything in unimaginable ways – making sense of new opportunities and adding immeasurable value to consumers and the planet. What shall we do with this insight?

What shall we build?

The marketing leader has a whole new stage upon which to imagine. Our imagination is the only barrier. We can add value in an increasingly new, different unexpected and as yet unbuilt place. These will be intelligent spaces, and we can go right ahead and build them if they don't exist.

The challenge for the marketer leader is to get out there. To out-imagine the competitor who hasn't thought far enough ahead about where all this leads next. And with the correct "purpose" the consumers are waiting to vote in your favor as they see the value and return on their involvement.

But as marketing leaders, we need to be curious and on top of what these innovations mean within our businesses and what ideas will fuel our futures and the new solutions we can bring.

Marketers are encouraged to master the impacts of personal data, privacy, and ethics. Issues that were never within their traditional domain. Now the realm embraces facial recognition, personal geo-tracking and for the business itself massive challenges around cybersecurity and the increasing cry for resilience post-COVID-19.

2020: Data is the New Oil

We hear a lot about data. We are surrounded by it. To understand the concepts and possibilities of what lies inside the data, we've had to build new machinery to deal with it.

Imagine the New Landscape

Quantum computers and AI are now terms on many business leaders' lips and will radically reshape the world, along with augmented reality. Google said its latest quantum computer had performed a calculation in 200 seconds that would take the fastest supercomputers about 10,000 years.

Imagine if you had the potential to accelerate the development of AI rapidly. What could/would you do?

AI systems can perform a wide range of tasks, from facial recognition and surveillance systems to autonomous activities. They can power abstract concepts that are simple to understand – from the pattern and anomaly detection to predictive analytics and conversational networks – that allow us to speak to devices and get beneficial results.

Soon, image, speech recognition and translation will allow us to avoid travel by enabling us to have real-time conversations with the entire world. Through machine learning, a critical dimension of AI, it's now possible to determine the emotional state of a human only by the way they walk.

Google is already using massively powerful computers to improve the software of self-driving cars. And because these new quantum machines operate using the same quantum properties as the molecules, they're trying to simulate it will mean more efficient products. These developments range from new materials for batteries in electric cars, through to better and cheaper drugs, vastly improved solar panels, and finding cures for our most frightening diseases.

These solutions will start to improve the systems we are operating within including predicting the financial markets, improving weather forecasts, and modelling the behavior of consumers in markets and their reactions to the messages we create as businesses.

Today's mature marketer can imagine a whole range of applications to identify future products and understand the motivations and whereabouts of their audiences.

Imagine the New Strategies

Any strategy that emerges from this has to involve critical thinking. Critical thinking will result in decision quality. Decision quality will power new marketing leaders.

In dynamic environments, decision-makers have to make sound judgments leading to new strategies. That requires quality time to pause and reflect, coupled with rapid access to relevant information. The lack of insight is often the biggest problem for most organizations.

Business leaders are likely to receive the information they need at different speeds. For example, they collect information quickly from technology, but slowly in other areas like customer feedback or employee engagement. So decision-making can only happen at the speed of the weakest link. Any successful strategy has to begin here. Organizations that are not well prepared with access to dynamic information will not fare well.

THE LEADERSHIP SINGULARITY FRAMEWORK

Shifting the Shape

The world either shapes us, or we shape it. Brands become leaders by shaping their marketplaces, and in the successful cases creating the market. And it's the stories we tell about ourselves and our organizations that have the most significant role in shaping them.

Shaping the Shift

For change to happen, we have to stop repeating past mistakes and define new territory. This has not been more true or life or death in our lifetime than right now. As we develop our new business territories, the rules that created the old ground need to be rewritten. If we can get all of this right, we have a once of a lifetime opportunity to change the world for the better.

The Old Ground – Pre-COVID-19

- People in business defined themselves through their function and job title. For example - "I am an accountant at XYZ company."
- Companies defined themselves through their products/services and occasionally could create a category defined by them (like hoover). For example, - "We make scanning devices."

Old business models are based on linear thinking:
What products? > Which markets? > How much investment? > What strategies?
Example: Scanning device product > hospitals, warehouses and delivery companies > $2M > distributors + marketing strategy

New Territories Post-COVID-19

The world has been through a period of enforced re-evaluation. Whether the change can be made to stick isn't clear yet; however, we've all seen a dramatic shift in pretty much every direction. Perhaps the most significant single hope is the revaluing of what we care about.

People in business can now define themselves through their interdependence and their intention – rather than their place on the organization chart.

Example: At XYZ company, I help the CEO, and other team leaders make educated financial decisions to support their teams for them to provide better solutions to our clients.

Companies now also define themselves through their interdependencies and intentions, but they're aligned to their mission.

Example: We help people in charge of data-collections to make sense of their data and give them more time to create value throughout their business.

The new business model is built on interdependence. There are more appropriate and different intentions which emerge within the Leadership Singularity Framework:

What purpose? > What intentions? > Who do we serve? > What is the impact? > How do we work? > How do we make it beautiful?

"We" Are the New Territories
Inward and Sacred Leadership

In coming to some simple conclusions within this book – the overarching factor is ourselves. No matter whether it's technological, political, economic, natural, or social challenges we are facing – we have to get ourselves ready first.

We've uncovered five business territories to deal with and have control over. We hope that the questions will guide you in your leadership endeavor and decision making.

FIVE PRACTICAL APPROACHES WITH FUNDAMENTAL PRINCIPLES

New Business Territory #1: Intention

- What is our genuine intention - the one that's driving our leadership desires?
- What is our purpose?
- What is that one aspect that ignites a passion in us and others?

As a leader, this is the raw material to understand and build from. We have to start with this authentic sense of self.

- Are we sincere when declaring it?
- Is it authentic and going to sustain us as the bullets come our way?
- Are we prepared to defend it - especially in the full glare of the old and traditional systems that preceded us?

- Are we prepared to alter everything in favor of a sincerely held purpose?
- Is this our intention? (Genuinely)

New Business Territory #2: Care
How does our purpose express itself in caring actions for others?

When trade was in its infancy, it was central to the life of any community. It fed, protected, and sustained everyone involved. It rested on a fair exchange – a bartering between people. In so many ways, the pandemic brought the idea behind these major exchanges back into focus.

It also brought into sharp relief how the (traditional) fair trading of marketplaces and communities got hijacked by people outside of the organizations. The hijackers didn't care about the community and focused only on the value that it could deliver – at any cost. The cost has been our humanity.

Care has made a comeback.
Whether it be the frontline healthcare workers or the small trader over the anonymous giant, the difference in the future will be defined by a currency of care – across all the stakeholders both inside and outside of the business.

How do we show that we care about others in our business practice and recognize others' value sharing the same resources?

New Business Territory #3: Consideration
Are we considering our place in a sustained future?

Thinking time is at a premium in the new age. One positive consequence of a global pandemic was to remind people of how insignificant we are in the grand scheme of things. We have a considerable effect as a species, and much of it is not good at all.

This book is as much about leadership as it is about mindset. A mindset that's just as critical in business and the marketing of it as it is in avoiding a climate catastrophe. Ignoring our fallibility is no longer optional.

We have to weigh abundance with scarcity, profit with purpose and convenience with fairness and equality. We have to give much more careful consideration to everything or we will fail.

Are we properly considering our business' impacts on people and the environment at large?

New Business Territory #4: Conditions
What are the conditions, systems and tools that we need to carry our intentions forward?

As a leader, we have the responsibility to create a different space, place and culture. This is so easy to say but will be the distinguishing feature of successful businesses.

Whether real world infrastructure and offices, or virtual and distributed, or a mixture of the two – creating the right conditions (i.e., measures, objectives, values, systems, processes and principles) will become a new and much-desired form of art.

What conditions are we creating through systems that empower our teams and communities?

New Business Territory #5: Beauty

How do we create a beautiful business, one that is creative, artistic, sensitive, and adaptable to the unknown and uncertainty?

Much is written about that which gets measured is what gets done. But this won't work so simply in the new interdependent massively entangled digital world.

Digital futures are also very human ones in which we will be encouraged to bring our humanity and emotions into the mix. We have to reframe the idea so that we can value both the science and the art* of what makes up the new business. Aaron Schwarztmann said, "art can only be created by people capable of certain kinds of social relationships".

In contrast, while we can get emotionally attached to our computers and other possessions, we feel no real empathy for their emotions, no ethical duty towards them, and no need to demonstrate our feelings toward them.

The business that will succeed will be beautiful because it will have both authenticity and integrity; both thoughtful and creative – a marriage of care and consideration and the right conditions to pursue the intention.

How can we create a safe space for our teams, to look at balance critically, compassionately, courageously, and make the change? **Let's go and do a beautiful thing**.

CHAPTER 6: WHO ARE THE CO-AUTHORS?

VIRGINIE GLAENZER

Co-founder and Storyteller, at AcornOak Agency.

Born and raised in Paris, France, I started my career in Sales in the technology industry. After moving to the US in 1998, I settled in the Francisco bay area with four suitcases and a head full of dreams. I co-founded three tech start-ups while beginning my journey to immerse myself in conscious leadership training in various disciplines such as psychology, wisdom traditions, awareness and mindfulness practices. I have harnessed more than 30 years of experience in digital marketing through executive leadership, consulting work, keynoting and thought leadership.

I moved to New York City in 2013 and became Vice President of Marketing for several organizations in technology, energy, and professional services. In my few years in the C-Suite, I've never found my place and I was even asked to leave twice despite outstanding customer results. I often was in misalignment with other executives who focused on business growth to the detriment of the customers. They were concerned about improving the bottom line, I was concerned about improving customers' lives. I started to sense a shift in society's values impacting marketing and online sales, which led me to write a short book "The Awakened Brand, Five Step for Creating an Awakened Brand by Tapping into The Consciousness Revolution."

Being extremely curious, I've always excelled at promoting emerging leadership trends and in 2019, I found myself launching AcornOak, a cooperative community powered by women of experience with a belief that the world is a better place when the feminine and masculine energy on the planet is more in balance.

When I'm not designing marketing and sales strategies or helping leaders navigate complexity with confidence and clarity of thought, I host the Podcast "**Pass The Mic**", which aims to bring compassion and conscious leadership to business and in our personal lives and help listeners ask themselves questions to become conscious self-authoring leaders.

For me, co-writing this book has been an improvisation act: I practiced navigating in the unknown without expectations, enjoying the journey and the blooming relationships while disrupting my own beliefs and knowledge.

JONATHAN COOK

For over 25 years, I've worked as an <u>independent researcher</u> of the culture of commerce. I do qualitative research, which means that I study ideas as ideas, without attempting to convert them into numbers.

As a child, I was fascinated by folklore. I loved the strangeness of it, the way that the stories people tell can feel true, even when the facts within them are obviously false. The myths and legends captured my attention, and the most important thing I learned in school at the time was that I wanted to follow my passions, rather than the assignments I was given by my teachers. I did just fine in school, but the educational experience felt tedious. The folklore I read in my own time seemed from a different world, one in which the characters were unmistakably alive.

For the first year after I graduated from high school, I attended classes at Xavier University in the city of Cagayan de Oro, on the island of Mindanao in the Philippines. I wanted to enter a foreign culture, to discover a place where folklore might still be alive.

What I found, of course, was a culture that, although it was foreign in some ways, was also surprisingly familiar. The Philippines, after all, had been a colony of the United States for decades, and life there, though different in many ways, was also thoroughly a part of the same modern world in which I had grown up.

I spent quite a while trying to look for the "real Philippines" underneath the modern experience. I wanted to sort out the American influence, and the Spanish influence that had come before that. It took me a long time to realize that what I was looking for wasn't the real Philippines at all, that the way that the Filipinos around me were living was the reality.

Returning to the United States, I studied anthropology in a continued quest for something that felt culturally authentic, something that could speak to the experience of feeling powerfully alive that I had found in mythological stories, but was more difficult to find in my actual life. I found that I enjoyed the process of the search for meaning in itself. Doing research was stimulating for me, as I found that even in the apparent rationality of our elaborately engineered modern life, there were odd cracks to be found, junctures of ideas that didn't match up neatly, revealing that people's lives weren't as logically planned as we like to pretend they are.

I found freedom within these cracks in the facade of rational modern life. It was in these in-between places that people could still move in unpredictable ways, feeling and creating unusual things. Discovering these strange open joints in conventional culture gave me the same enjoyable space to breathe that I felt in my time between classes, the same vitality I had read of in the folklore I explored as a child.

After I left school, I continued my work as a researcher. Under the mentorship of a psychologist, I learned methods of immersive interviewing designed to allow the expression of the emotions that people ordinarily suppress. I branched out into broader, deeper, slower methods of qualitative inquiry, informed by the classic ethnographic approaches of anthropologists, but studying the strange beliefs and behavior hidden behind the mask of rationality in commercial culture rather than seeking the exotic in a faraway community,

I have found that people remain, despite all their efforts to fit in with the mechanistic models of industrial society, richly, thickly, and warmly weird. Our marketplace behavior doesn't follow the rules of logic. Our feelings don't match what we know we ought to think. We hunger for something more than what is profitable.

Over a quarter-century of work, the research I've done for corporations, nonprofits, and governmental agencies has revealed that the age of myth and ritual isn't something of the past. It hasn't been destroyed by the materialism of commercial culture. To the contrary, the weird paths of folklore form the warp and woof of the fabric of the marketplace, explaining the strange, everyday deviations from economists' models of rational transactions driven merely by price, convenience, and rote habit.

I have discovered that, if you take the time to actually be with people for a while, to watch what they do and listen to what they have to say, you'll find that there is a legacy of profound human meaning hidden within the most apparently mundane products, services, and experiences. We're still creating myths and enacting rituals. It's simply one of the taboos of modern commercial culture to acknowledge that's what we're up to.

My job is to ask questions. Every question is a quest. Together, our job is to listen, to find the path that echoes our questions in response.

JOHN CASWELL

Head of Crayons at the Group Partners.

A few years ago I came upon an expression that summarizes my life well. *"May the bridges I burn light my way."* I get asked what it means so many times.

We are all the product of our experiences but we should never be a slave to them. What happened is no precursor to what may happen. We need to have zero expectation and maximum preparedness for anything to occur.

Each time I moved on the prior experience suggested a fresh path. It lit my way and I never look back. Now we've written a book on the subject. From a strict private military school to illegal substance fueled art school. A DJ by night and a budding idiot by day.

Eventually, I landed in a proper job. Friends of mine had inadvertently created the UK's most successful microcomputer manufacturer. It was a wild and very privileged ride. I was partly implicated in massive success and eventually had to watch as it exploded into dismal failure.

Little did I realize at the time but we had spawned and were building another business within the business. And that became the most successful business ever in this country: $32 Billion. Long after I left the firm they were responsible for the core chips in the majority of the world's mobile phones. It's still pretty outstanding.

But the bridge needed burning. The city lights shone brightly. I had to leave it all behind because the promise of a shiny corner office with my name engraved on it and a few more horsepower in my car sounded the death knell. It signaled a kind of conformity that I didn't need.

I left it all to form my own Ad agency in London. Eventually, I sold it to one of the big global holding companies and having set fire to that one I've been clean for two decades.

I decided to use all my insight and a visual approach in order to create the future for global clients. I bring them the path into the light.

I do it because I know how terribly difficult it is to drive change in anything. I like to think that each one of these situations, and the countless miniature situations within them, that I learned. I doubt I did full justice but I like to think.

Being involved in pulling this book together has been another real privilege – lighting the way to yet another new beginning. It was a great opportunity to stand our concepts up to scrutiny and see it dramatically improved by my colleagues.

I've already put many of these combined ideas into practice. So much more will emerge through this collaboration. As we've said earlier, this book wasn't caused by the pandemic, but it was certainly reshaped by it.

By way of summarizing the experience of these collected works and collaborative energies, some clear themes have emerged for me.

Marketing, by the updated definition in this book, has been changed for good. Only the future will judge whether we were right. Marketing will be understood to be the mentality needed to survive the future and not a job function.

Whatever the idea, product, socially critical change to be made, service, solution, business, government, nation or thought experiment – if it can't be defined, be ethical, be moral, told simply and the audience persuaded then its stillborn.

Leadership can be taught as long as humans can be made to think and believe systems and values changed. If not these leaders will have no followers and ideas will never make it through alive.

The new marketer is the new leader. The new leader is the new marketer. Leaders won't be able to lead unless they understand the importance of marketing and how to execute in the singularity that represents.

Attention is the new black. Gaining the attention of the public required a global pandemic. With that attention came hope and promises of never going back to normal.

Therefore, the challenge now will be keeping that attention once there's a remedy.

Personally, my life's crusade has been to try to make people think. To use whatever means at my disposal to get people to stop what they've always done, long enough to realize that the world around them has changed and there is most likely a better way.

Everything about our project was a wake-up call. As we were starting the work we had a bigger wake-up call. It made our wake up call even more important. If the new skills needed by the marketing leader weren't clear before then they had better be now.

PATRICK NOVAK

Founder and Chief Empowerment Officer at <u>Trident Strategies</u>.

I was born in Bethesda, Maryland into a Navy family. Due to the proximity of military culture, I became fascinated by the prospect of service. The patriotism, teamwork, and desire to protect fueled my drive to pursue this goal. My very supportive family put me through the best education, leadership and athletic programs that anyone would be lucky to have, and I'm forever grateful for that. This excellent preparation served me well as I graduated from the <u>United States Naval Academy</u>, and went on to pursue Naval Aviation (or so I thought).

I enjoyed Flight School and was selected to fly helicopters, but my heart wasn't in it. I transitioned out of the Navy after leading a few programs and entered the void. Searching for purpose after being part of something that big wasn't easy. It was humbling. I sold what little I had and wandered with a motorcycle and backpack, power-washing sidewalks at night to eat. Yes, after receiving the best education in the nation and most amazing leadership experience in the world, I found myself cleaning up trash in CVS parking lots at 3 AM for cash. I had amazing friends that helped me and they'll always be in my heart until its final beat. So, maybe you're wondering how the hell I escaped defeat?

After enough time had passed, I returned to the Washington DC area and reintegrated into the Defense Contracting community. I worked with many CEOs and leaders to grow their companies. As connectivity expanded, I served on boards, privately consulted clients on Middle Eastern affairs and won millions in government contracts. Throughout this time, I consistently noticed a chasm across countless companies.

I witnessed an untenable void in leadership that was not only destroying productivity and profit but also the lives of employees. Maybe being knocked down in life a few times myself, combined with the unforgettable leadership lessons from the Naval Academy created the perfect storm for me to passionately fight against negative corporate dynamics and put people first.

This shift in energy resulted in the creation of **Trident Strategies**. A leadership consulting firm with an edge to cut quickly towards solutions for clients in the Federal market. Turns out we were onto something by putting humans first, because nothing would challenge our leadership model more than a global health crisis that crippled the economy, and magnified our faults and worst practices like never before. Seems like the perfect time to write a book, right?

Just weeks before the pandemic, Virginie Glaenzer invited me to contribute leadership inputs for this very book she was producing. I had no idea it would turn into a self-help and practical psychology guide to advise companies on how to completely rethink a more sustainable business model.

To our welcome surprise, the themes we were presenting just prior to the pandemic have aligned seamlessly with new strategies we're presenting to our clients right now, in response to COVID-19.

The best way to honor this book is to widely share the excellent thought leadership from authors Virginie, Jonathan, and John. While only four deep, we represent the diversity of thought and experience that is commonplace in corporate America. Our group had pure motivation for collaboration and that's where I found this work to be very emblematic of my own ethos. That being, in order to drive out negativity (or any cultural sickness) from a system – people must come together and agree upon the threats, be well equipped with the truth, and offer an alternative value system that equally serves both employees and corporations alike.

I'll always be positive for a better future and hope you feel the same after using this book to take a pragmatic pause and evaluate what matters most in life, the other humans with which we share this beautiful world.

FINAL THOUGHTS

NEW BUSINESS CRAFTSMANSHIP
FOR CHAOTIC TIMES

JOHN CASWELL

I will take away from writing this book during the crisis a number of things. More respect than ever for the incredible imagination and human creativity that it has sparked. Every one of them represents the new concepts of marketing leadership.

The crisis itself saw the return to the small local provider that managed to spin up an e-commerce and delivery system to bring properly fresh and farm-grown goodness to the door far better than the big players who failed to reward my years of loyalty.

For the marketer/leader they can start to see how it generates creativity that can create positive change. There may well be booms in things like digital healthcare and tracking solutions alongside telemedicine and other methods of prevention.

Put this trigger together with a new attitude to health there will hopefully be a rise in antidotes to the misinformation infodemic - beware the deep fakes. Mental health issues are going to be a negative side effect of this plague and marketing leadership should be dialed in to help.

I've been working virtually for a decade so writing the book as a collaboration was a joy. The virtual technology and behavior were normal to me but now many more people are used to it and that's forced new habits and more confidence.

There's been a blurring of time and behavior – things are becoming acceptable over Zoom that we're not in the traditional contexts of the business meeting. Thank goodness in some ways - fatigue and longing for the old ways for others.

Things may well change permanently in terms of crazy travelling schedules that may well alter a lot of people's working practices for good. Distributed teams working in flexible formats. The hollowing out of our cities, those that we will deeply miss and those that will come back refreshed and renewed with purpose.

We can already see more challenges to the norms and standards of a fixed infrastructure – bringing the freedom to work appropriately (given the new-found ability to use multiple channels/platforms) to adapt to the context of the moment.

The word hybrid will be applied to countless things. We are already bringing supply chains nearer to home – stopping the inequities that exist within them and reducing harm to the planet. We need to make shipping cheap stuff around the world because we can - unacceptable unless it is sustainable and ethically done.

New models have been trialed and applied that would never have been applied or tested before. This has forced people to try ideas. To try things out is good and we couldn't have hoped for some of these trials before.

Real-time hiring of people and skills for gaps in capability as an example – all of it achieved remotely, digitally. I heard someone say the resistance to digital is evaporating. What organizations resisted for a decade is now core to survival and innovation. Let's hope it stays so.

Online access as a human right. And beyond that two words that seem to sum it all up for me. Appreciation of the things that matter and perspective. The appreciation of mental health and emotional wellbeing.

PATRICK NOVAK

My top two takeaways from this book are:

1. **Honest Leadership will set you free.** You must approach every area of your life with a strong sense of leadership and responsibility for all within your sphere of influence. The temperament, tone and intent with which you guide other humans have a massive impact on our collective purpose, passions and existence. When crisis or panic hits, the most important job for those in charge – is to first be in charge of themselves so they can show others the way forward as well. The best way to do that is to be honest with ourselves so that in turn we'll be honest with our team, customer, and community. Telling the truth when times are tough is hard, but if you do – it will pay off tremendously when everything returns to smooth sailing.

2. **Your team's time is everything.** Time is the only asset on the planet that offers the exact same availability and value equally to all of humanity, no matter your charter in life. You can do everything you can to maximize your time, but you can't exchange it, buy it back or manipulate it. Given that this is the case, it's everyone's unique responsibility to live in such a way that we respect not only how we spend our time, but most importantly the time of those in our workforce. In order to do this – we owe them a new

depth of creative thinking to chart a future that puts our people first. This is not easy, and it will alter our financial models, but it will return dignity and purpose back to the corporate environment that has been fading away quickly into the night. It's time to do what's right and employees will deeply appreciate that you're putting them first in the fight.

How can you practically apply this book during a crisis?

After you've had time to absorb the high-level themes, pull your partners and employees in for a conversation around the new ideas proposed in this book. Explore the implications and identify positive ways your firm can contribute to a more honest and sustainable business model that puts leadership-driven marketing as a core capability for everything you do.

Given that your business only exists to improve the lives of your customer, start to model every internal practice as a vehicle to drive external service. This shift to a more inclusive partnership not only strengthens your customer bonds but also empowers your staff to really know that their functions are not just part of the company's success – but more importantly critical to your success.

JONATHAN COOK

For generations, students of business have been taught that marketing is a science. It has been supposed that marketing can be measured and managed like a machine.

The only problem with this approach is that the goal of marketing is to influence human behavior, and humans are not computers with legs. We are not rational problem-solving devices. We are hungry, playful animals living in unpredictable times.

At the beginning of 2020, self-appointed business futurists made confident predictions about the year to come. The prophets at QuantumRun predicted that a robotic exoskeleton to help elderly people move would become widely available for purchase.

Nicholas Badminton advised that 2020 would be defined by a controversy over geoengineering.

Futurum predicted that by the end of this year, artificial intelligence capabilities for understanding human conversation would make touch screens unnecessary for most apps.

IBM foretold that in 2020, AI capabilities would require employers to redefine job roles, requiring human workers to focus on acquiring new professional skills

The Wall Street Journal predicted that this year's stock market performance would be modestly bullish, accompanied by a broader economic expansion.

Michelle Ruiz interviewed trend forecasters and concluded that "The 2020s are moving towards a bit more of a respite, something that's more optimistic."

None of them predicted the COVID-19 pandemic. Whether or not they were equipped with the most powerful supercomputers and most sophisticated predictive algorithms, no one in business foresaw the impact of the coronavirus in time to take meaningful action to prevent the global economic catastrophe.

The business mythology of the last decade was centered around the idea that data processing would save the world. Digital technology, it was said, was enabling business leaders to make accurate predictions and take agile responses. Machine learning algorithms would tell us what to do.

This year, the data-driven business has been caught flat-footed. Supply chains quickly broke down. Information infrastructure buckled under new, unanticipated demands. Months into the crisis, there was still no consensus about where the crisis was going, and when it might be ending.

The humbling lesson of 2020 for business leaders is that we don't know as much as we thought we knew. Our information technologies are not as robust as we thought they were. Uncertainty overwhelms our scientific management. The consequences of our overconfidence are cruel. Trillions of dollars have been spent to prop up fragile business systems, and yet, even this massive public support of private enterprise appears to have been insufficient. Bankruptcies abound, and those businesses that survive are laying people off by the millions.

The first decades of this century have seen the growth of a cult of optimization that, like cancer that has metastasized to the bones, thins out the organizational skeleton of business to the point of minimum viability, until it is barely able to hold up the musculature of operations. When an unexpected challenge comes along, the bones of the self-scavenged corporate structure snap. Efficiency has made business brittle.

Bold leaders will pursue a different kind of optimization, one that seeks opportunities to invest, rather than deplete. Extractive models of business have created a degenerate world, but it's not too late to turn things around. Marketing can become a regenerative process, but only if it directs our attention back into the world, rather than distracting us from it.

Marketers can no longer afford to play games with the abstractions of operationalized data. Instead of floating above the world, collecting data from it, and using glorified calculators to construct elaborate models of how people ought to behave, business leaders need to get grounded in the humanity of enterprise.

The corporate campuses of glass and steel stand empty. The human economy remains open for business. Let's set up shop there.

VIRGINIE GLAENZER

For many years, I believed the definition of Marketing to be the one taught in my MBA as the *"growth engine of business to increase shareholders values'*.

I was wrong. *"When the system is no longer driving sustainable results for profits, for the people and for the planet, it becomes inept and corrupted." Extract* Chapter Two. We've collectively asked. *"If marketing is no longer the growth engine, what is its purpose?"*

I have been asking myself the same question and searching for answers was an experience that Joseph Campbell describes well: *"The cave you fear to enter holds the treasure that you seek."*

In light of the new role and responsibilities of The Leadership Singularity, it requires a dramatic shift for one to find new personal alignment. I will not quit the art of storytelling and sensemaking but continue to expand my understanding of others through the practice of regenerative economics to restore my faith in marketing leadership.

In this collective writing experience, I've discovered that being in the flow of uncertainty is a way to open space for meaning creation. Today, I understand leadership as a process that requires constant movement and fluidity in space and time.

My desire is to be on a stage of uncertainty to create the conditions for others' journey to find their own meaningful experience with a belief that the world is a better place when the feminine and masculine energy on the planet is more in balance.

From status and power, marketing leadership has become a singularity alive, in flux and creating space for others to enter and have a meaningful experience *to them*.

To find my own way out of our embodied economic crisis narrative as a marketer and a leader, it will only be superseded by my ability to welcome visitors into my house to create a belonging feeling.

WHAT'S NEXT?

HOW MARKETING CAN SAVE THE WORLD

If you are interested in exploring the questions below, we invite you to join our circle of thinking practitioners.

- Can we still grow while encouraging people to consume less?
- Who would we be if we relinquished the concept of "crushing the competition"?
- What would a truly humane economy look like?
- Could we create bigger/broader systemic change if we invited allies?
- Is there such a thing as good materialism?
- Could our operating nature be seasonal like nature?
- What is it that is actually, asking to be mourned, for the threshold to be crossed?
- How can we find the courage to trust?
- How do we live with more intentionality?
- How do we create enough attention for anything to be understood enough so as to be engaged long enough to make any difference?
- Can we teach these new ideas to the future generations in ways that they improve and make them more a part of our natural behavior?

Click here to join us. www.acornoak-studio.net, is creating a platform to empowers everyone to become self-authoring leaders and a podcast to challenge the status quo.

REFERENCES

Page 10

https://www.brandwatch.com/blog/amazing-social-media-statistics-and-facts/

Page 16

https://www.forbes.com/sites/stevedenning/2017/11/30/why-the-world-is-getting-better-why-hardly-anyone-knows-it/#1984d1ce7826

https://awealthofcommonsense.com/2018/04/50-ways-the-world-is-getting-better/

https://ourworldindata.org/literacy

https://www.theatlantic.com/ideas/archive/2019/08/whys-it-so-awkward-to-say-the-economy-is-great/595408/

Page 19

https://hbr.org/2017/01/survey-peoples-trust-has-declined-in-business-media-government-and-ngos

Page 24

https://corpgov.law.harvard.edu/2019/02/06/the-wells-fargo-cross-selling-scandal-2/

Page 28

https://hbr.org/2019/12/can-you-know-too-much-about-your-organization

https://www.forbes.com/sites/williampesek/2020/05/07/wework-downfall-means-adam-neumann-should-sue-himself/#5d7c12614da0

Page 30

https://whatis.techtarget.com/definition/black-hat-SEO
https://searchitchannel.techtarget.com/definition/keyword-stuffing

https://whatis.techtarget.com/definition/patent-troll

https://whatis.techtarget.com/definition/patent

Pages 36-41

https://www.challengergray.com/press/press-releases/2020-january-ceo-turnover-report-219-leave-their-posts-more-new-ceos-come

https://g8fip1kplyr33r3krz5b97d1-wpengine.netdna-ssl.com/wp-content/uploads/2020/04/Navigating-the-Coronavirus-infodemic.pdf

https://www.govexec.com/management/2020/01/no-1-obstacle-great-workplace-culture/162580/

Pages 87-98
https://www.acornoak.net/

https://www.amazon.com/Awakened-Brand-Virginie-Glaenzer-ebook/dp/B017VE8KVS/ref=sr_1_1?dchild=1&keywords=virginie+glaenzer&qid=1587995044&sr=8-1

https://www.acornoak.net/pass-the-mic-podcast

http://jonathancook.us/

https://www.grouppartners.online/

https://www.tridentserves.com/

https://www.usna.edu/homepage.php

Page 111
www.acornoak-studio.net

Made in the USA
Columbia, SC
22 October 2020